Cosy Christmas
COLLECTION

Featuring 15 crochet patterns for you to add a handmade touch to the Holidays and crochet your very own cosy Christmas

Published in the United Kingdom in 2024

© Fiona Field | Cosy Rosie UK, 2020-2024

All rights reserved. No part of this book may be reproduced, copied, displayed, distributed or adapted in any way, with the exception of certain activities permitted by applicable copyright laws, such as brief quotations in the context of a review or academic work.
The designs contained in this book and the items created from them are for personal use only.
Commercial use of either the designs or items made from them is strictly prohibited.
For permission to publish, distribute or otherwise reproduce this work, please contact the author at fiona@cosyrosieuk.co.uk

The Author can accept no legal responsibility for any consequences arising from the application of information, advise or instructions given in this publication.

ISBN 978-1-0687794-3-5

A CIP catalogue record for this book is available at the British Library

Contents

Introduction … 1

Get Set for Success

Materials & Tools … 2
- Video Tutorials
Reading Written Patterns … 3
Check your tension … 5
Finishing Off … 6

Tips & Tricks

Invisible Join … 7
Invisible decrease … 7

Dress the Tree

Granny's Christmas Bauble … 9
Mini Santa Hat's … 11
Candy Cane Reindeer … 12
Mini Stocking Garland … 14
Holly & Berries Stocking … 17
Snazzy Chevron Tree Skirt … 25

Character Cuties

Simon the Snowman … 28
Gary the Gingerbread … 32
Terry the Tree … 35

Festive Homeware

Terry the Tree Cushion … 39
BIG Bauble Cushion … 40
Santa Napkin Ring … 44
Santa Gift Basket … 46
Christmas Tree Coaster … 52
Christmas Tree Mug Cosy … 55

Introduction

I love Christmas and the holiday season. I love gifting to those that I love and welcome any opportunity to be creative with my decor that get's put up as soon as it's socially acceptable!

Every bauble on my tree has a memory attached; from where it was purchased, or who made it for me. The joy I feel unwrapping each one is one of my holiday highlights.

Designing crochet for the holidays is something I can't resist. Every year I release 2-3 more holiday inspired patterns to spread the joy and inspire others to add a special handmade something to their home.

Since 2018, I've hosted in-person workshops for absolute beginners through to workshops focused on more advanced techniques, all while I also sold my finished projects at craft fairs and via online retailers.

When things had to be put on hold at the start of 2020, I had to find new ways to share my love of crochet, and I made the decision to publish the patterns I'd designed for my finished projects, so that others could enjoy the craft and make them too.

Since then, I've published over 150 patterns and also share YouTube video tutorials sharing crochet techniques and offering extra support to help people complete my designs, and the joy I feel sharing this craft with others is like nothing else!

Let's start with the pattern details and then how to read a pattern so you can get stitching up your very teapot cosies.

Get Set For Success

Whether you are new to the craft or a seasoned pro, it's always good to start at the very beginning, and set ourselves up with everything we need to complete our projects.

Over the next few pages, you will find a list of the materials needed which include all the tools recommended to use during these projects along with details on how to read a crochet pattern and stitch up your very own Cosy Christmas.

You'll also find an abbreviation list that includes all the basic stitches used. Details on the specific materials used, yarn amounts, and how to complete any special stitch instructions will be found with the pattern they are used in.

Materials & Tools

YARN
All of the patterns in this book can be made using either animal or synthetic fibre yarns such as wool or acrylic; I used acrylic yarn for each pattern.

The patterns are written using different yarn weights including:
- DK/Size 3
- Aran/Size 4
- Chunky/Size 5

and each pattern will state which yarn weight to use, along with the recommended hook size.

Where multiple colours are used in a pattern, they will be labelled using letters so you can recreate the same look.
For example:
- **A** - Fuchsia
- **B** - Light pink
- **C** - White

TOOLS
- 4mm crochet hook
- 5mm crochet hook
- 6mm crochet hook
- scissors
- darning needle

Shopping list of extras

The patterns will advise all specific materials needed to complete the project.
The extra items are:
- pom-pom maker - size 35mm
- 6cm shatterproof bauble
- 1cm googly eyes
- candy canes
- 7mm black pom-poms
- 7mm pom-poms in bright colours
- 2cm red pom-poms
- glue gun and glue sticks
- toy stuffing
- 9mm safety eyes
- 2" black buttons
- 3" wooden ring
- 14" round cushion pad
- 7mm invisible snap fasteners

Video Tutorials

Some of the patterns have a video tutorial available to follow along to - scan the QR code to be taken to the Playlist

Reading Written Patterns

This book has only written patterns so familiarising yourself with the abbreviations will help you to translate the instructions in the crochet patterns.
It's recommended to take time to read through a whole pattern before beginning, to ensure you understand the abbreviations and special stitches used in a pattern.

Abbreviations

US Terms	
st(s)	stitch(es)
ch	chain
ch sp	chain space
sl st	slip stitch
sc	single crochet
sc2tog	single crochet decrease
hdc	half double crochet
hdc2tog	hdc decrease
dc	double crochet
tr	treble crochet
TC	turning chain
MC	magic circle
RS	right side
WS	wrong side
YO	yarn over hook

Alongside these basic stitches, you will see other abbreviations for special stitches that will be explained above the pattern where the special stitch is used, along with instructions on how to complete the stitch.

* - ASTERISKS
An asterisk is used to mark a point within a pattern or row where the stitches are repeated. You may be asked to repeat from * to end or for a number of times as stated in the instructions.

[ ] - SQUARE BRACKETS
Square brackets are used to indicate when an instruction should be repeated or multiple stitches should be worked into the same stitch or chain space.

( ) - ROUND BRACKETS
Round brackets are used to give additional instructions e.g (does not count as st) and may also be used give additional stitch counts when there are multiple sizes included in a pattern.

A, B, C - CAPITAL LETTERS
Capital letters are used in place of a yarn shade name. See Yarn in Materials & Tools for an example.

Let's put that knowledge into practice with this example row of pattern instructions, written in the abbreviated form:

Row 2: With **B**, ch 1 (does not count), sc in next 2, *ch 5, skip 2, sc in next 3; repeat from * to last 4, ch 5, skip 2, sc in last 2, turn - 5 ch-5 sps, 16 sc

Here's the full version of the abbreviated instructions:

Row 2: Using shade Light Pink, make 1 chain (the chain of 1 does not count as a stitch), single crochet into the next 2 stitches, * make 5 chains, skip the next 2 stitches, single crochet into the next 3 stitches; repeat from * to the last 4 stitches of the row, make a chain of 5, skip the next 2 stitches, single crochet into the last 2 stitches, turn - after completing the row, the stitch count will be 5 chain 5 spaces and 16 single crochet stitches

When you become familiar with the abbreviations, your mind will fill in the missing words and translate the abbreviations almost instantly making reading patterns much quicker.

US and UK Terms

The different between UK and US terms can create an additional challenge - **this book is written in US terms.** To show some of the differences, below you can see the US abbreviations plus the equivalent UK term.

US Term		UK Term		
st(s)	stitch(es)	st(s)	stitch(es)	
ch	chain	ch	chain	YO, pull through loop on hook
sc	single crochet	dc	double crochet	Insert hook into st, bring up loop, YO, pull through both loops
hdc	half double crochet	htr	half treble crochet	YO, insert hook into st, bring up loop. YO, pull through all through loops
dc	double crochet	tr	treble crochet	YO, Insert hook into st, bring up loop, YO, pull through 2 loops, YO, pull through 2 loops
tr	treble crochet	dtr	double treble crochet	YO twice, insert hook into st, bring up loop (4 loops on hook) [YO, pull through 2 loops] 3 times

Check your Tension

Tension and Gauge can be scary words when learning how to crochet. In fact, many crocheters just wing it when it comes to checking their tension. For some patterns like these, we can almost get away without checking our tension matches the pattern, as you can check the finished size as you make. It's more important to keep your tension is consistent throughout, and make sure you stitches are not too loose, especially in the Character Cuties.

What is Gauge?

Gauge is simply the number of stitches and rows created by the designer within a 10cm/4 inch square.

A pattern will tell you the recommended hook size and the stitch used to create your own gauge swatch to check your tension matches and achieve the correct finished size by following the pattern.

If you were to use a different weight yarn or hook size to make your project, and you didn't meet the gauge in the pattern, the finished size would be different to what the pattern states.

Each of the patterns will state a finished size, or a to fit size.

Adjusting your Tension

Too Big?
If your finished project is too big, you can swap your hook out for a smaller hook and your stitches will be smaller.

Too Small?
If your finished project is too small, blocking may relax the stitches enough to achieve the correct finished size - check by gently stretching the finished tea cosy around a filled pot. The heat from the water will relax the stitches.

If that doesn't help, you can remake the tea cosy using a larger hook to make the stitches bigger.

Tension Top Tip
I'm a huge fan of using a centre pull from a ball - that way the ball stays in one place and no extra tension on the yarn is created as you crochet.

Finishing Off

Before you've even started, let's learn how to create the perfect finish! Some of the patterns will be sewn together to complete the projects, but some will just need to be finished off. Let's start with the most important stage of finishing - fastening off.

Fastening Off

Before you cut that final strand of yarn in your project, it's important to fasten off the yarn securely. This will help secure your project.

The most secure way to fasten off any project is to create a chain 1 after you've completed your final stitch by:

1. Yarn over the hook
2. Pull the yarn through the loop on your hook
3. Cut the yarn at least 6 inches away from the hook to create a tail for weaving in the ends - *look out for instructions for leaving long tails for sewing up*
4. Pull the loop up until all the remaining yarn and the cut end has passed through the loop on your hook

Weaving in Ends

Weaving the ends in securely is an important part of creating a great finished project that you can be proud of:

1. Thread the end tail of yarn on to a darning needle
2. Working on the wrong side of your project, weave the needle through the back of the stitches, or under the loops of the previous stitches for at least 2 inches
   a. If weaving a different colour, check the needle can not be seen on the right side of your project
3. Pull the needle and yarn through where you've weaved
4. Repeat steps 2-3 in the opposite direction, 2 more times

Top Tip

- Work through the plies (strands) of the yarn when weaving for a more secure weave

Tips & Tricks

Here are 2 tips and tricks that you can use in some of these patterns that will help to give your crochet projects a perfect finish.

Invisible Join

Once you have mastered this technique, you can apply it to finish almost all of your projects making weaving in the final end simple, easy and almost untraceable!

Traditionally, when we finish of a row or a round, we would make a ch 1 after completing the final stitch, then pull the working yarn through the chain to create a little knot.

Instead:
- **DO NOT** join with a slip stitch to the beginning of the round
- Leaving your hook in the stitch, cut the yarn, leaving enough to weave in your ends
- Pull the working yarn through the final stitch
- Thread the yarn on to your darning needle and insert your needle under the 1st stitch of the round from front to back, and pull the needle and yarn through
- Insert your needle through the the middle of the last stitch completed, and out under the back loop of the stitch
- Weave in your end to finish the project

Invisible Decrease

Learning how to do an invisible decrease will completely change the finish to your crochet toys.

The standard sc2tog can leave a hole where there shouldn't be and the invisible decrease eliminates this hole.

The invisible decrease can be used in any crochet pattern that is worked in the round, with the right side of your project facing you, and where you are instructed to decrease the stitch count by 1, such as Gary the Gingerbread or Simon the Snowman.

How to crochet an invisible decrease
1. Insert your hook under the front loops only in the next 2 stitches
2. YO, bring up a loop, through the front loops of both stitches
3. YO, pull through the 2 loops on the hook to complete the invisible decrease

Granny's Christmas Bauble

This pattern can be used to cover up those less loved, basic baubles and transform them into a crochet masterpiece that matches the rest of your holiday decor.

You can adjust the pattern for larger baubles by working additional rounds of Round 4, or using a heavier weight yarn and corresponding hook size.

Pattern Notes

- Bauble is made by making 2 pieces in joined rounds that are then joined together
- Beginning ch 1 **DOES NOT** count as a stitch
- Beginning ch 3 **COUNTS** as dc
- It is recommended to fasten off each round

Finished Size

To fit a 6cm bauble
- To measure your bauble, place it between 2 flat objects and measure between to ensure the correct size

Materials

- DK (Size 3) acrylic or cotton in various shades
- I used Paintbox Yarns Simply Cotton DK, 100% cotton, 50g/125m in the shades:
    - **A** - Paper White (401)
    - **B** - Red Wine (416)
- 4mm crochet hook
- scissors
- 6cm shatterproof bauble

Pattern

Make 2

Round 1: With **A** MC (or ch 4, sl st to 1st to create a ring), ch 3 (counts as dc), *working into centre of ring*, 11 dc, sl st to top of ch 3 to join -12 dc
Fasten off

Round 2: Join **B** between any post (*not in a st*), ch 3, dc in same as ch 3, 2dc between each post around, sl st to top of ch 3 to join - 12 2dc
Fasten off

Round 3: Join **A** between any pair of 2dc, ch 3, 2dc in same as ch 3, 3dc between each 2dc around, sl st to top of ch 3 to join - 12 3dc
Fasten off

Round 4: Join **B** between any 3dc group, ch 3, 2dc in same as ch 3, 3dc between each 3dc around, sl st to top of ch 3 to join - 12 3dc
Fasten off

Round 5: Join **A** in any st, ch 1 (does not count), sc in same as ch 1 and each st around, sl st to 1st to join - 36 sc
Fasten off with a long tail for sewing
Weave in all ends except tail from Round 5

Sewing Up

- With **RS** facing, position to create bauble shape
- place the 2 tails from Round 5, 1 stitch apart
- using 1 of the remaining tails and working through back loop only on both panels, sew together until 8 sts remain to be sewn
- insert bauble and position top of bauble to the tail not being used to sew up
- continue to sew remaining sts, working through back loop only to the to top of bauble
- secure each tail with a knot at the side of the top of the bauble
- weave remaining ends

Mini Santa Hat's

These mini Santa Hats can be hung on the tree, or used as an egg cosy to create a festive theme to any breakfast.

Pattern Notes

- This pattern is worked in the round from top down
- Project is worked holding **2 stands of yarn** together
- Ch 1 at the beginning of the rounds **DOES NOT** as a stitch

Finished Size

- 4" circumference or to fit a medium chicken egg

Materials

- DK Acrylic yarn in 2 colours
- I used Paintbox Yarns Simply DK in
    - **A** - Pillar Red (114) - 15m
    - **B** - Paper White (100) - 10m
- 4mm Crochet hook
- Pom-pom maker - size 35mm
    - I used Clover Pom-Pom Maker
- Tapestry needle
- Scissors

Pattern

Round 1: With 2 strands of **A**, make a MC (or ch 4, sl st to 1st ch to create ring) ch 1, 6 hdc into centre of ring, sl st to 1st hdc to join - 6 hdc

Round 2: Ch 1 (does not count), 2hdc in same as ch 1 and each around, join - 12 hdc

Round 3: Ch 1, hdc in same as ch 1, 2hdc in next, *hdc in next, 2hdc in next; repeat from * around to end, join - 18 hdc

Rounds 3-5: Ch 1, hdc in same as ch 1 and each around, join - 18 hdc

Round 6: With **B**, ch 1, *working in BLO*, sc in same as ch 1 and each around, join - 18 sc

Round 7: Ch 1, *working to BLO*, sc in same as ch 1 and in each stitch around, join using invisible join (see page 7)
Weave ends, leaving beginning tail to secure pom-pom

Finishing Off

Make a small pom-pom with **B**
Thread long tails from pom-pom through top of the Mini Santa Hat and tie securely to beginning tail of Hat

To create a loop for hanging, thread 1 strand **B** on to yarn needle and thread needle through rear of hat, underneath pom-pom and tie a knot.

Candy Cane Reindeer

Add a tasty treat to the Christmas tree with reindeers that have edible antlers made with candy canes. You can substitute the candy canes with 2-tone chenille sticks if you'd like to make this pattern less sugary.

Pattern Notes

- Reindeer is worked in a continuous spiral
- It is recommended to place a stitch marker in the 1st stitch of the round and move the marker up as you progress through the pattern
- Reindeer is worked holding **2 stands of yarn** together

Materials

- 2 strands of DK (Size 3) Acrylic yarn
  - I used Hayfield Bonus DK 100% acrylic, 100g/280m in shade Taupe
- 5mm Crochet Hook
- Darning needle
- Scissors
- 1cm (10mm) Googly eyes
- 2cm fluffy pom-poms
- Glue gun

Pattern

Round 1: Holding 2 strands of yarn, ch 7, sc in 2nd ch from hook and next 5, *rotate to work on other side of beginning chain,* sc in next on other side of beginning ch, sc in each to end, **do not join** - 11 sc

Rounds 2-12: sc in each around - 11 sc

Adding the Hanging Loop

- Fold the Reindeer flat in line with the base to create sides
- sc in each st around to the middle of the 1st side
- ch 8, sl st to same as beginning of ch

Fasten off, weave in ends

Making it a Reindeer

Position the eyes and pom-pom as preferred and secure with a small amount of hot glue

Mini Stocking Garland

These cute mini stockings can be hung individually on the tree, or joined together with a chain, slip stitching the hanging loop of the stockings to the chain at regular intervals, and create a stunning garland to string across your fireplace.

Pattern Notes

- Toe & leg section are worked in a continuous spiral
- Heel is worked in rows which are seamed to join
- Beginning ch 1 **DOES NOT** count as a stitch

Finished Size

6" from top of loop to toe when made with DK and 4mm hook

To create larger stockings, use Aran/worsted weight yarn and a 5mm crochet hook

Materials

- 35m DK (size 3) acrylic yarn
    - I used WI Premium Acrylic, 100% acrylic (100 g/250m) in 2 shades:
        - **A** - White
        - **B** - Red
- 4mm crochet hook
- Scissors
- Needle

Pattern - One Colour Stocking

Toe - *worked in continuous rounds*
It is strongly recommended to use a stitch marker to keep track of 1st stitch when working in continuous rounds

Round 1: Make MC (or ch, 4 sl st to 1st to create ring), 10sc into centre of ring, **do not join** - 10 sc

Round 2: 2sc in each around - 20 sc

Rounds 3-11: sc in each around - 20 sc (9 rounds)
DO NOT fasten off

Heel - *worked in turned rows*

Row 1: Ch 1, sc in next 10, leave remaining sts unworked, **turn** - 10 sc

Rows 2-6: Ch 1, sc in each across, turn - 10 sc
DO NOT fasten off

Seaming Heel
- Fold in half, with **WS** facing (folding the **RS** together), ch 1, working through both layers of Row 6, sl st in each across (5 sl st)
- Fasten off and weave ends
- Turn Heel **RS** out

Leg - *worked in continuous rounds*

Round 1: With **RS** facing, join yarn in 1st unworked st after Heel seam, ch 1, *working around in row ends of Heel and continuing around top of Round 11 of Toe*, sc in each st around - 22 sc

Rounds 2-12: Sc in each around - 22 sc (11 rounds)

Round 13: Sc in each around to in line with Heel seam, ch 15, sl st to same to form hanging loop
Fasten off, weave ends

Now you've mastered the One Colour stocking, let your imagination go wild with the colour combinations.

You can opt for bold and bright stockings, changing colour every 2 rows, or use the colour suggestions with the One Colour stocking.

Jogless Colour Change when Working in the Round

To minimise colour change while in the round, complete the last YO of the stitch in the new colour and replace the 1st stitch of the round with a slip stitch in the new colour.

Two Colour Stocking

Work pattern as One Colour Stocking, changing colours in the following rows:
Toe
Rounds 1-3: With **A** (white)
Rounds 4-11: With **B** (red)

Heel in **A**

Leg
Rounds 1-9: With **B**
Rounds 10-13: With **A**

Multicolour Stocking

Work pattern as One Colour Stocking, changing colours in the following rows:
Toe
Rounds 1-3: With **A** (white)
Rounds 4-5: With **B** (red)
Rounds 6-11: Continue to change colour every 2 rounds

Continue to **Heel** in **A**

Leg
Rounds 1-2: With **B**
Rounds 3-4: With **A**
Continue to change colour every 2 rounds
Continue to **Round 13** in **A**

Holly & Berries Stocking

The Holly & Berries Stocking allows you to practice lots of different crochet techniques, including how to turn a heel, and using posts stitches to create a diamond pattern to create an heirloom that can be hung on the fireplace year after year.

This pattern is worked top down to the toe, and there are 2 versions of the Leg section which have different crochet skill levels. One is perfect for beginners and the other is a more advanced pattern that uses posts stitches to create a diamond pattern across the top of the leg.

Pattern Notes

- This pattern is worked 4 parts:
  - Leg
  - Heel
  - Foot
  - Toe
- The Leg and Foot sections are worked in rows
- The heel is worked in short rows
- The Toe is worked in a continuous spiral
- Beginning ch 1 **DOES NOT** count as a stitch
- Beginning ch 3 **DOES** count as a stitch
- Ch 1 of Berry st in **NEVER** worked in, be sure to skip this ch when working row after berry rows
- It may be helpful to place markers into each sl st until you are comfortable skipping the ch-1 of the Berry st

Special Stitches

Berry = Berry stitch
- YO, insert hook in next st, YO, pull up loop, YO, pull through 1st loop on hook.
- YO, Insert in same, YO, pull up loop, YO, pull through 1st loop on hook.
- YO, pull through 5 loops,
- Ch 1

FP tr = front post treble crochet
- YO hook 2 times, insert hook around stitch indicated, YO, pull up loop,
- [YO, pull through 2] 3 times

FP tr2tog = front post treble 2 together
- YO hook 2 times, insert hook around stitch indicated, YO, pull up loop,
- [YO, pull through 2] 2 times
- YO 2 times, insert hook around next indicated, [YO, pull through 2] 2 times,
- YO, pull through remaining 3 loops

hdc3tog = hdc decrease across 3 sts
- [YO, insert hook into next, YO, bring up loop] 3 times
- YO, pull through all 4 loops

Materials

- 160m chunky, arcylic yarn
  - I used Hayfield Bonus Chunky, 100% acrylic (100 g /3.5 oz. 137m/150yds) in 2 shades:
  - **A** - Signal Red
  - **B** - White
- 6mm crochet hook
- Scissors
- Needle

Finished Size

Total Length - 18" by 6" wide

Pattern - Simple Leg

Row 1. WS: With **A,** Ch 40, sc in 2nd ch from hook and each ch across, turn - 39 sc

Rows 2-3: Ch 1 (does not count as st), hdc in each across, turn - 39 hdc

Row 4: Ch 1, sc in same, *Berry in next, sl st in next; repeat from * across, turn - 19 Berry st, 1 sc, 19 sl st

Row 5: Ch 1, sc in same, skip ch-1, *sl st in next Berry, sc in next sl st, skip ch 1; repeat from * to end, working sc in last, turn - 20 sc, 19 sl st

Row 6: Ch 1, sc in same, sl st in next, *Berry st in next sc, sl st in next; repeat from * across to last st, sc in last, turn - 18 Berry st, 2 sc, 19 sl st

Row 7: Ch 1, sc in same, sc in sl st, skip ch-1, *sl st in next Berry st, skip ch 1, sc in next sl st; repeat from * across to end working sc in last, turn - 21 sc, 18 sl st

Rows 8-9: Ch 1, hdc in each across, turn - 39 hdc

Rows 10-11: Ch 1, sc in each across, turn - 39 sc

Row 12: Ch 3 (counts as dc), dc in each across, turn - 39 dc

Row 13: Ch 1, sc in each st across, turn - 39 sc

Rows 14-15: Repeat Row 12-13

Rows 16-17: Repeat Rows 10-11

Rows 18-19: Repeat Rows 8-9

Rows 20-26: Repeat Rows 4-10
Fasten off, leaving long tail for sewing up
With **WS** facing, seam using whip stitch
Continue to Heel

Pattern - Advanced Leg

Rows 1-12: work Rows 1-12 as Simple Leg

Row 13: Ch 1, sc in same, sc in next 2, working around 2nd and 5th sc 2 rows below, FP tr2tog, *sc in next 3, starting around same as last and skipping 3 sts between 2 rows below, FP tr2tog; repeat from * across to last 3, sc in last 3, turn - 9 FP tr2tog, 30 sc

Row 14: Ch 3, dc in each across, turn - 39 dc

Row 15: Ch 1, sc in same, working around FP tr2tog 2 rows below, FP tr, *sc in next 3, starting around same as last and next FP tr2tog, FP tr2tog; repeat from * across to last 4, sc in next 2, FP tr around same as last FP tr2tog, sc in last, turn - 8 FP tr2tog, 2 FP tr, 29 sc

Rows 16-17: Repeat Rows 10-11 as Simple Leg

Rows 18-19: Repeat Rows 8-9 as Simple Leg

Rows 20-26: Repeat Rows 4-10 as Simple Leg
Fasten off, leaving long tail for sewing up
With **WS** facing, seam using whip stitch

Pattern - Heel

The heel is worked in short rows meaning that the last stitch is worked into the row attached to the leg of the stocking, and the remaining stitches are left unworked and the stitch count increases by 1 with each row worked

Row 1: With **B** and **RS** facing, counting from seam, join in 9th stitch, ch 1 (does not count as st), sc in same, sc in next 8, skip seam, sc in next 10, turn - 19 sc

Row 2: Ch 1, sc in same, sc in next 11, leaving remaining 7 sts unworked, turn - 12 sc

Row 3: Ch 1, sc in same, sc in next 5, leaving remaining 6 sts unworked turn - 6 sc

Row 4: Ch 1, sc in same, sc in next 5, sc in next st 1 row below (indicated by needle), turn - 7 sc

Row 5: Ch 1, sc in same, sc in next 6, sc in next st in row 1 row below, turn - 8 sc

Rows 6-14: Repeat Row 4
Number of stitches worked before working additional sc, 1 row below on leg will increase by 1 with each row worked ending with a total stitch count of 17 sc at end of Row 14

Row 15: Ch 1, sc in same, sc in next 16, sc in next st in row 1 row below, sl st to next st on leg, turn - 18 sc, 1 sl st

Row 16: Ch 1, skip sl st, sc in next 18, sc in next st in row 1 row below, sl st in next st on leg - 19 sc, 1 sl st
Fasten off, weave ends

Pattern - Foot

Worked in turned rows

Row 1: With **A**, and **RS** facing, join yarn in 10th st of heel, ch 1, sc in same and next 9, skip sl st, sc in next 18 sts, skip sl st, sc in next 9, **turn** - 37 sc

Row 2: Ch 1, sc in same, sc in next 7, hdc3tog, sc in next 15, hdc3tog, sc in next 8, turn - 31 sc, 2 hdc

Row 3: Ch 1, sc in each across, turn - 33 sc

Row 4: Ch 1, sc in same, *Berry in next, sl st in next; repeat from * across, turn - 16 Berry st, 1 sc, 16 sl st

Row 5: Ch 1, sc in same, skip ch-1, *sl st in next Berry, sc in sl st, skip ch 1; repeat from * to end working sc in last, turn - 17 sc, 16 sl st

Row 6: Ch 1, sc in same, sl st in next, *Berry st in next sc, sl st in next; repeat from * to last st, sc in last, turn - 15 Berry st, 2 sc, 16 sl st

Row 7: Ch 1, sc in same, sc in sl st, skip ch 1, *sl st in top of Berry st, skip ch 1, sc in sl st; repeat from * to end working sc in last, turn - 17 sc, 16 sl st

Rows 8-9: Ch 1, hdc in each across, turn - 33 hdc

Rows 10-13: Repeat Rows 4-7

Row 14: Ch 1, hdc in each across, turn - 33 hdc

Row 15: Ch 1, sc in each across - 33 sc
Fasten off, leaving long tail for sewing
With **WS** facing, seam using whip stitch

Pattern - Toe

Worked in continuous rounds, recommended to place marker in 1st stitch

Round 1: With **B** and **RS** facing, join in 1st st after foot seam, ch 1, sc in same and each around - 33 sc

Round 2: Sc in each st around - 33 sc

Round 3: [Sc in next 8, sc2tog] 3 times, sc in last 3 - 30 sc

Round 4: [Sc in next 7, sc2tog] 3 times, sc in last 3 - 27 sc

Round 5: Sc2tog, *sc in next 3, sc2tog; repeat from * around - 21 sc

Round 6: *Sc in next 2, sc2tog; repeat from * to last st, sc in last - 16 sc

Round 7: Sc2tog 8 times - 8
Fasten off, using tail to weave through remaining stitches to close

Pattern - Hanging Loop

Hanging Loop

Row 1: With **A** and **RS** facing, join in top of leg in st before seam, ch 20, starting in 2nd ch from hook, sc in each back loop of ch, sl st to same as ch 20, turn - 19 sc

Row 2: Ch 1, sc in each across - 19 sc

Fasten off, leaving long tail for sewing loop, sew unattached end of loop to inside of leg to complete loop
Weave remaining ends

Fringing for Simple Leg

- Cut 39 10" lengths with **B**
- With **RS** facing, insert hook into st in Row 9
- Fold 1 strand in half and bring through
- Pull ends to secure
- Repeat across Row 9

Snazzy Chevron Tree Skirt

This design looks stunning when worked in 2 or more colours - how to space the colours out them is completely up to you - change colour every 2 rows, 4 rows, or even every row, for a really bold look!

Pattern Notes

- This pattern is worked in turn rows before edging the sides
- Beginning ch-3 **DOES** count as stitch
- Designer changed colours every 2 rows

Take a moment to go through the pattern and highlight the stitch counts for the size being made, which will be written in order: 20" (42", 48", 56")

Materials

- Any worsted /Aran weight acrylic yarn.
    - I used Paintbox Yarns Simply Aran 100% Acrylic (100g (3.5oz), 184m (201 yds)) in the following 2 shades:
        - **A** - Pillar Red (214)
        - **B** - Paper White (200)
- Designer made 42" skirt and used 600m in **A** and 400m in **B**
- 5mm crochet hook
- Scissors
- Tapestry needle

Finished Size

- 20" for table top trees
- 42" for 4-6 foot trees
- 48" for 7 foot trees
- 56" for 7.5 foot and taller trees

The size is measured from edge-to-edge, across the middle of the skirt when laid flat, from peak to peak

Pattern

Row 1: With **A**, ch 25, sc in 2nd and each across, turn - 24 sc

Row 2: Ch 3 (counts as st), dc in same, 2dc in each across, turn - 48 dc

Row 3: Ch 3, dc in same, *skip next, dc in next, (dc, ch 2, dc) in next (peak made), dc in next; repeat from * to last 3, skip next, dc in last 2, turn - 48 dc, 11 ch-2 peak sps

Row 4: (INC) Ch 3, dc in same, skip next, dc in next 2, (2dc, ch 2, 2dc) in ch-2 peak sp, dc in next, *skip next 2 sts, dc in next, (2dc, ch 2, 2dc) in ch-2 peak sp, dc in next; repeat from * to last 3 sts, dc in next, skip 1, 2dc in last - 72 dc, 11 ch-2 peak sps

Note - *begin changing colours every 2 rows*

Row 5: (INC) With **B**, ch 3, dc in same, skip 2, dc in next 3, (2dc, ch 2, 2dc) in ch-2 peak sp, dc in next 2, *skip 2, dc in next 2, (2dc, ch 2, 2dc) in ch-2 peak sp, dc in next 2; repeat from * to last 4 sts, dc in next, skip 2, 2dc in last - 94 dc, 11 ch-2 peak sps

Row 6: (No INC) Ch 3, dc in same, skip 2, dc in next 4, (dc, ch 2, dc) in ch-2 peak sp, dc in next 3, *skip 2, dc in next 3, (dc, ch 2, dc) in ch-2 peak sp, dc in next 3; repeat from * to last 4 sts, dc in next, skip 2, 2dc in last - 94 dc, 11 ch-2 peak sps

Rows 7-14 (30, 36, 42): Repeat Rows 4-6 continuing to change colour every 2 rows
Do not fasten off
Continue to Edging & Ties

Understanding the Pattern Repeat

Number of stitches between ch-2 peak spaces and troughs will increase by 1 after each **(INC)** row worked, with the additional stitches worked into the peak. The stitch count will increase by a total of 24 sts across the row.

Repeat Example
Rows 7: (INC) Ch 3, dc in same, skip 2, **dc in next 4**, (2dc, ch 2, 2dc) in ch-2 peak sp, dc in next 3, *skip 2, dc in next 3, (2dc, ch 2, 2dc) in ch-2 sp, dc in next 3; repeat from * to last 4 sts, dc in next, skip 2, 2dc in last, turn - 116 dc, 11 ch-2 peak sps

Note - *as there was no increase in Row 6, there is no change to the number of stitches worked up to the peak in Row 7 - marked in bold above*

Row 8: (INC) Ch 3, dc in same, skip 2, dc in next **5**, (2dc, ch 2, 2dc) in ch-2 sp, dc in next **4**, *skip 2, dc in next **4**, (2dc, ch 2, dc) in ch-2 sp, dc in next **4**; repeat from * to last **4** sts, dc in next, skip 2, 2dc in last, turn - 138 dc, 11 ch-2 peak sps

Note - *The increases are only worked in the ch-2 peak sp in the (INC) rows. The increase stitch count between ch-2 peak sp & trough are marked in bold above in Row 8 and below in Row 9, as the repeat is worked in Row 8, the increase will be seen in Row 9*

Row 9: (No INC) Ch 3, dc in same, skip 2, dc in next **6**, (dc, ch 2, dc) in ch-2 sp, dc in next **5**, *skip 2, dc in next **5**, (dc, ch 2, dc) in ch-2 sp, dc in next **5**; repeat from * to last **6** sts, dc in next, skip 2, 2dc in last, turn - 138 dc, 11 ch-2 peak sps

Edging & Ties

Round 1: *Rotate to work across row ends across side edges of skirt,* ch 1, 2sc evenly across each row end to top of skirt and beginning ch, *rotate to work in other side of beginning ch,* sc in other side of each ch around, *rotate to work across row ends in side of skirt*, 2sc evenly across each row end
Fasten off, weave ends

Ties
Beginning in top, side edge of skirt, working down the side:
- Join **A**, in 1st sc, *ch 40, fasten off
- Rejoin in same as last st worked
- Repeat from * every 5 rows to create 2 (5, 6, 7) ties
- Repeat on other side of skirt

Weave all remaining ends

Simon the Snowman

A white Christmas is the thing of dreams - with the chances always low, Simon will help make your dreams come true and allow you create your own snowman. All without the need to get cold.

Pattern Notes

- This pattern is worked in 4 parts:
    - Body and Head - worked continuous rounds
    - Hat - worked continuous rounds
    - Scarf - worked in turned rows
    - Arms - worked in turned rows
    - Nose is worked in turned rows
- It is recommended to place a marker in the 1st st of the continuous rounds and moving up with each round worked

Materials

- Aran/Size 4 yarn 100% acrylic yarn
- I used Lovecrafts Simply Aran 100% acrylic (100g/184m) in the following shades
    - **A** - 50 m in White Paper White
    - **B** - 10m in Red yarn for scarf plus scrap for smile
    - **C** - 5m in Orange
    - **D** - 10m in Black
    - **E** - 15m in Brown
- 5mm crochet hook
- stitch marker
- scissors
- tapestry needle
- 3 3mm black pompoms for buttons
- 1 pair of 9mm safety eyes
- glue gun

Finished Size

- 8" tall including Hat

Body

Round 1: With **A**, make MC (or ch 4, sl st to 1st to create ring), *working into centre of ring*, 8 sc, pm in 1st sc, - 8 sc

Round 2: 2sc in each around – 16 sc

Round 3: *sc in next, 2sc in next; repeat from * around – 24 sc

Round 4: *sc in next 2, 2sc in next; repeat from * around – 32 sc

Rounds 5-8: sc in each around – 32 sc

Round 9: *sc in next 2, sc2tog across next 2; repeat from * around – 24 sc

Round 10: sc in each st around – 24 sc

Round 11: *sc in next, sc2tog across next 2; repeat from * around – 16 sc

Round 12: sc in each st around – 16 sc

Round 13: *sc in next, sc2tog across next 2; repeat from * around to last 4, sc in last 4 – 12 sc
Stuff body firmly

Head

Round 1: Continuing in **A**, *sc in next, 2sc in next; repeat from * around – 18 sc

Round 2: *sc in next 2, 2sc in next; repeat from * around – 24 sc

Rounds 3-5: sc in each around – 24 sc
Secure safety eyes between Rounds 4-5, 3 stitches apart

Round 6: *sc in next 2, sc2tog across next 2; repeat from * around – 18 sc

Round 7: *sc in next, sc2tog across next 2; repeat from * around – 12 sc

Round 8: *sc in next, sc2tog across next 2; repeat from * around – 8 sc
Stuff remainder of Body & Head
Fasten off leaving long tail for weaving
Weave through front loop of each st and cinch closed, weave ends

Scarf

Row 1: With **B**, ch 38, sc in 2nd ch from hook and each across - 37 sc
Fasten off, weave ends

Nose

Row 1: With **C**, ch 4, sc in 2nd from hook and next, sl st in last, ch 2, sl st in same as last, *working through 1 loop of st and beginning ch*, sl st in each across to last, sc in last, sl st to same as last
Fasten off with long tail for sewing
Sew to the head one row below and in between the eyes

Hat

Round 1: With **D**, make MC (or ch 4, sl st to 1st to create ring), *working into centre of ring*, 8sc, pm in 1st sc, - 8 sc

Round 2: 2sc in each around – 16 sc

Round 3: sc in each around - 16 sc

Round 4: *working in BLO,* sc in each around - 16 sc

Rounds 5-6: Repeat Round 3

Round 7: *working in FLO,* *sc in next, 2sc in next; repeat from * around - 24 sc

Round 8: *sc in next 2, 2sc in next; repeat from * around - 32 sc
Fasten off, weave ends
Sew to top of head using another strand of **D**

Arms

Make 2
Row 1: With **E**, ch 6, sl st in 2nd ch from hook and each across - 5 sl st
Fasten off with a long tail for sewing

Smile - using scrap of **D**, create a smile under the eyes - use photo as guide

Secure scarf around neck and sew 1 Arm between Rounds 11-12 on each side of Body, trim beginning tails to create sticks for fingers

Using glue gun, secure 3mm pom-poms down the middle of body

Gary The GingerBread Man

The smell of the warm spices when the gingerbread men go into the oven creates a festive joy. With this easy crochet pattern, you can stitch up your own Gary and keep that festive cheer with you year round.

Pattern Notes

- This pattern is worked in 3 sections:
    - Head and Body - worked together in one piece
    - Legs - worked directly on to the body
    - Arms - worked separately and then attached
- Each section is worked in a continuous spiral, without joining the rounds
- It is recommended to place a stitch marker in the first stitch of each round and move the marker up as you progress on to the next round

Materials

- 40m DK/size 3 acrylic yarn with 3mm hook
- 1 pair of 6mm safety eyes

or

- 40m Aran/size 4 acrylic yarn with 4mm hook
    - I used Paintbox Yarns Simply Aran, 100% acrylic (100g,184m)
- 1 pair of 9mm safety eyes

- 6" of red yarn for smile
- toy stuffing
- 3mm pom-poms for the "sweets"
- stitch marker
- scissors
- Yarn needle
- Hot glue or fabric glue
- 1m red double faced satin 3mm ribbon

Optional - rust proof pins

Finished Size

- 9cm tall with DK
- 14cm tall with Aran

Head & Body

Round 1. RS: Make MC (or ch 4, sl st to 1st ch to create ring), 6sc into ring, pm into 1st st made – 6 sc

Round 2: 2sc in each st around – 12 sc

Round 3: *sc in next, 2sc in next; repeat from * around – 18 sc

Round 4: *sc in next 2, 2sc in next; repeat from * around – 24 sc

Rounds 5-7: sc in each around – 24 sc
Secure eyes between Rounds 5-6, with 3 stitches between eyes

Round 8: *sc in next 2, sc2tog across next 2; repeat from * around – 18 sc

Round 9: *sc in next, sc2tog across next 2; repeat from * around – 12 sc

Round 10: Repeat Round 9 – 8 sc
Stuff the head firmly, ensuring eyes are not misaligned by stuffing

Round 11: 2sc in each around to last, sc in last – 15 sc

Round 12: *sc in next 2, 2sc in next; repeat from * around to last, sc in last – 20 sc

Rounds 13-22: sc in each around – 20 sc
Fasten off

Lightly stuff the body, leaving room to work around base of body (once the 1st leg is complete, the body can be firmly stuffed)

Legs

Place your hook in the centre stitch, in line with the middle of the eyes and through to the other side of the body, ensuring there are 9 stitches either side of your hook to create equal leg openings

Round 1: Join yarn through both edges of Body, *working around from centre st,* 9 sc around to end, pm in 1st st made – 9 sc

Rounds 2-6: sc in each around to end – 9 sc

Round 7: [sc2tog across next 2 sts] 4 times to last, sc in last – 5 sc
Stuff leg lightly ensuring body is completely stuffed too

Fasten off, leaving long tail for weaving
Use long tail to weave through each st to close
Weave ends

Repeat from Round 1 to create 2nd leg, joining in same beginning point as 1st leg

Arms

Arms - make 2
Round 1. RS: Make MC (or ch 4, sl st to 1st ch to create ring), 4 sc into ring, pm into 1st st made – 4 sc

Round 2: 2sc in each around – 8 sc

Rounds 3-8: sc in each around – 8 sc

Fasten off, leaving long tail for weaving
Use long tail to weave through each st to close
Weave ends

Flatten arms and pin into position each arm between Round 2-3 on opposite sides of the body before sewing into position

Using red yarn, create a smile under the eyes - use photo as guide

Tie a bow around neck using red ribbon

Using hot glue (or fabric glue), secure the mini pompoms down the front of the body and ribbon between the head and body

Use a strand of yarn and thread through head to create a hanging loop if required

Terry the Tree

'Tis the season to celebrate all things festive; the lights, the treats and of course the trees! As you can see from his happy smile, Terry the Tree loves the season of goodwill as much as we do!

Pattern Notes

- This pattern is worked in 2 parts:
    - 2 tree shapes with trunk worked in turned rows that are stuffed and sewn together
- Star is worked in a joined round and sewn onto the tree
- Beginning ch 1 **DOES NOT** count as stitch

Materials

- 100% cotton yarn
- I used Rico Creative Cotton Aran, 100% Cotton (50g/85m) in the following shades:
    - **A** - Fir Green
    - **B** - Cinnamon
    - **C** - Yellow
- 4mm crochet hook
- Red acrylic yarn
- 2 9mm safety eyes
- Toy stuffing

Finished Size

- 6 inches tall by 3 inches wide

See the Terry the Tree Cushion to create a larger version of this pattern

Pattern - Tree

Make 2

Row 1: With **A**. ch 19, sc in 2nd ch from hook and in each across, turn - 18 sc

Row 2: Ch 1 (does not count as st), skip 1st stitch under ch 1, sc in next and each across, turn - 17 sc

Row 3: Ch 1, skip 1st stitch under ch 1, sc in next and each across, turn - 16 sc

Rows 4-10: Repeat Row 3 - the stitch count will decrease by 1 on each row to 9 sts remaining at the end of Row 10

Row 11: Ch 1, skip 1st stitch under ch 1, sc in next and each across, ch 4, turn - 8 sc, 4 ch

Row 12: Sc in 2nd ch from hook and next 2 ch, sc in each across, ch 4, turn - 11 sc, 4 ch

Row 13: Sc in 2nd ch from hook and next 2 ch, sc in each across, turn - 14 sc

Row 14: Ch 1, skip 1st stitch under ch 1, sc in next and each across, turn - 13 sc

Rows 15-27: Repeat Row 14 - the stitch count will decrease by 1 on each row until 1 st remains at the end of Row 14
Fasten off leaving a 20" long tail for sewing

Pattern - Trunk

Row 1: Counting from beginning of last row worked on tree, join **B** in 8th stitch, sc in same st as joined and next 3, *leave remaining sts unworked*, turn - 4 sc

Row 2: Ch 1, sc in same as ch 1 and each across, turn - 4 sc

Row 3: Ch 1, 2sc in same as ch 1, sc in next 2 sts, 2sc in last st, turn - 6 sc

Row 4: Ch 1, sc in same st as ch 1 and each across - 6 sc
Fasten off with a 12" tail for sewing
Repeat for other tree shape

- Affix safety eyes between Rows 6-7, leaving 3 sts between each eye on one the tree panels
- With red yarn, secure a cute smile in the row below the eyes, leaving 3 sts between, using cover photo as guide
- Sew 2 trees together from the top point down, across top of trunk and back to top point, stuffing lightly before completing the sewing up
- Sew the Trunk together on each edge using brown yarn tail

Pattern - Star

Round 1: With **C**, ch 6, sl st to 1st to create a ring, ch 1, *working into centre of the ring*, *hdc, dc, ch 2, sl st to 1st ch, dc, hdc, sl st to ring; repeat from * a further 4 times to create a 5 point star
Fasten off with a 12" tail for sewing

Sew Star on to the Terry to complete your tree

Terry the Tree Cushion

If you love Terry the Tree, why not make him supersized! This pattern recreates Terry in the form of a cushion; perfect for those afternoons spent on the sofa watching Christmas movies

Pattern Notes

- This pattern is worked in 2 parts:
    - 2 tree shapes with trunk worked in turned rows that are stuffed and sewn together
    - Star is worked in a joined round and sewn onto the tree
- Beginning ch 1 **DOES NOT** count as stitch

Materials

- 100% cotton yarn
- I used Rico Creative Cotton Aran, 100% Cotton (50g/85m) holding 2 strands together in the following shades:
    - **A** - Fir Green
    - **B** - Yellow
- 6mm crochet hook
- Red acrylic yarn
- 2 2" black buttons
- Toy stuffing

Finished Size

- 13" tall and 12" at widest point

Pattern

Make 2

Row 1: With 2 strands of **A**, ch 37, sc in 2nd ch from hook and in each across, turn - 36 sc

Row 2: Ch 1 (does not count as st), skip 1st stitch under ch 1, sc in next and each across, turn - 35 sc

Row 3: Ch 1, skip 1st stitch under ch 1, sc in next and each across, turn - 34 sc

Rows 4-19: Repeat Row 3 - the stitch count will decrease by 1 on each row to 18 sts remaining at the end of Row 19

Row 20: Ch 1, skip 1st stitch under ch 1, sc in next and each across, ch 5, turn - 17 sc, 5 ch

Row 21: Sc in 2nd ch from hook and next 2 ch, sc in each across, ch 5, turn - 17 sc, 5 ch

Row 22: Sc in 2nd ch from hook and next 2 ch, sc in each across, turn - 21 sc

Row 23: Ch 1, skip 1st stitch under ch 1, sc in next and each across, turn - 20 sc

Rows 24-42: Repeat Row 23 - the stitch count will decrease by 1 on each row until 1 st remains at the end of Row 42
Fasten off leaving a 30" long tail for sewing

- Affix buttons for eyes between Rows 14-15, leaving 6 sts between each eye
- With red yarn, secure a cute smile in the row below the eyes, leaving 6 sts between, using cover photo as guide
- Sew 2 trees together from the top point down, across the bottom, and back to top point, stuffing lightly before completing the sewing up

Pattern - Star

Round 1: With 2 strands of **B**, ch 6, sl st to 1st to create a ring, ch 1, *working into centre of the ring*, *hdc, dc, ch 2, sl st to 1st ch, dc, hdc, sl st to ring; repeat from * a further 4 times to create a 5 point star
Fasten off with a 12" tail for sewing

Sew Star on to the Terry to complete your tree

BIG Bauble Cushion

This giant bauble is just as snuggly as the Terry the Tree Cushion, and another chance to make a statement piece for your couch.

Pattern Notes

- This pattern is worked in continuous rounds, with all 4 colours worked in the same round
- Beginning ch 1 does **NOT** count as stitch
- Please be aware of colour change indications - the colour changes are **NOT** only made at the start of the round
- Placing stitch markers in 1st stitch of each round, and working loop of colour not being used, is recommended

Materials

- Chunky/Bulky size 5 yarn
- I used Hayfield Bonus Chunky 100% Acrylic yarn in the following shades
    - **A** - Red (75m)
    - **B** - White (75m)
    - **C** - Red (75m)
    - **D** - White (75m)
    - **E** - Yellow (30m)
- 6mm Crochet Hook
- 14" round cushion pad
- Fibre fill (toy stuffing)
- Scissors
- Tapestry needle
- Optional Bauble Loop
    - 2 or 3 inch wooden ring - designer used inside of embroidery hoop
    - **E** - Yellow (20m)

Changing Colours

To change colour during each round it is recommended to pull up a large loop after last stitch worked before colour chance, or secure with a lockable stitch marker before placing loop of next colour on hook and continue in next stitch

Pattern

Make 2

Round 1. RS: With **A**, ch 4, sl st to 1st to create ring, *ch 1 (does not count as st), [sc, 3 hdc] in ring, *place marker in working loop*, join next colour; repeat from * with **B**, **C** and **D** - 1 sc, 3 hdc in each colour

Round 2: With **A**, *2hdc in next, hdc in next, 2hdc, leave remaining st unworked, *place marker in working loop, pick up next colour*; repeat from * with **B**, **C** and **D** - 5 hdc per colour

Round 1	Round 2

Round 3: With **A**, *2hdc in next, hdc in next 3, 2hdc in next, leave remaining st unworked; repeat from * with **B**, **C** and **D** - 7 hdc per colour

Rounds 4-15: Repeat Round 3. The number of stitches to work between 2hdc in each colour will increase by 2 sts with each round worked. At the end of Round 15 there will be a total stitch count of 31 hdc per colour

Round 16: With **A**, *sc in next 31, leave remaining st unworked; repeat from * with **B**, **C** and **D** - 31 sc per colour

Round 17: With **A**, *sc in next 31, leave remaining sc unworked; repeat from * with **B**, **C** and **D** - 31 sc per colour

1st Panel: Fasten off all colours, weave ends

2nd Panel: Continue to Joining

Joining

Position panels **WS** together, with 2nd panel on top
Align matching colours as follows:
- **A** loop (Red) in line with last stitch of **D** (White), so **A** is worked over **B**, and **B** is worked over **A** etc

Round 1: *working through both panels,* join using flat slip stitch join, changing colours when next loop is reached
Insert cushion pad before last colour change worked
Fasten off, weave remaining ends
Continue to Bauble Top

Flat Slip Stitch Join

Important things to remember when creating a flat seam:
- Work with the right side of your project facing
- Insert hook through BLO of chain/stitch, from the front to back
- Keep yarn to the back of the project at all times

With **RS** facing:
- insert hook through back loop of 1st panel
- insert hook into the front loop (loops closest to you) of 2nd panel from the front (right side) of the panel to the back (inside of the cushion *(3 loops on hook)*
- YO with working yarn, pull through both panels and loop on hook to slip stitch and join

Repeat sl st join around, working through BLO of front panel and FLO of back panel to next colour loop, changing to next colour loop to continue spiral pattern

Bauble Top

Round 1: With **E**, ch 6, 2hdc in 2nd ch from hook, hdc in next 3, 3hdc in last, *rotate to work other side of beginning ch,* hdc in next 3, hdc in last, join - 12 hdc

Round 2: Ch 1, 2hdc in same and next, hdc in next 3, 2hdc in next 3, hdc in next 3, 2hdc in last, join - 18 hdc

Round 3: Ch 1, 2hdc in same and next 3, hdc in next 5, 2hdc in next 4, hdc in next 5, join - 26 hdc

Round 4: Ch 1, *working in BLO,* hdc in each around, join - 26 hdc

Rounds 5-8: Ch 1, hdc in each around, join

Round 9: Ch 1, *working in FLO,* *(sc, hdc, ch 2, sl st to 1st ch, hdc, sc) in next, sl st in next 2; repeat from * to end, on last repeat sl st to next st only - 9 peaks

Hanging Loop

Round 1: Join **E** to wooden ring, ch 1, sc around ring to cover, join to 1st st, fasten off, leaving long tail for sewing

Sew hanging loop to top and middle of Bauble Top to secure

Santa Napkin Ring

Adding a touch of the festive season doesn't need to be complicated - this simple napkin ring is quick and easy to make, so even with 12 coming round for the main meal of the holidays, you can have these stitched up in next to no time!

Pattern Notes

- The napkin ring is worked in joined rows
- To minimise colour change while in the round, complete the last YO of the stitch in the new colour

Finished Size

- 6" circumference, 2.5" wide

Materials

- 35 yds of Aran/Worsted weight yarn in 3 shades
    - I used Brava Worsted, 100% acrylic (100g = 218yds) in following 3 shades
    - **A**- White - 10 yds
    - **B**- Red - 15 yds
    - **C**- Black - 15 yds
- Plus scraps Yellow - 1 yds
- 5mm crochet hook
- Scissors

Pattern

Round 1: With **A**, ch 23, sl st to 1st ch to create ring, ch 1, sc in each around, join - 23 sc

Rounds 2-4: With **B**, ch 1, sc in each around, join - 23 sc

Rounds 5-6: With **C**, ch 1, sc in each around, join - 23 sc

Rounds 7-9: With **B**, ch 1, sc in each around, join - 23 sc

Round 10: With **A**, ch 1, sc in each around, join - 23 sc
Fasten off, weave ends

With scraps of yellow, sew Buckle between Rounds 5-6, using picture as a guide

Santa Gift Basket

There is something overly festive about Santa, and I have quite the collection of Santa's that are displayed every year in my home. This cute Santa storage pot is perfect as a table decoration, to store tasty treats or even to use as a small gift basket!

Pattern Notes

- This pattern is worked in 2 pieces; Lid and Base which are both worked in the round
- The eyes, nose and mouth are embroidered onto the pot
- Beginning ch-1 does **NOT** count as stitch
- The optional fluffy element is worked through the front loop using the surface crochet technique

Materials

- Any Aran/Worsted weight acrylic yarn
- I used Brava Worsted Weight Yarn (100% Acrylic - 218yds/100g) in the following 5 shades:
    - **A** - Red - 150m
    - **B** - Blush - 20m
    - **C** - Black - 10m
    - **D** - White - 75m
    - **E** - Caution - 30cm
- 4mm crochet hook
- Scissors
- Tapestry needle

Optional - to make Santa's Beard Fluffy

- Sirdar Snuggly Snowflake Chunky (100% Polyester, 25g 68yds) - 17m

Changing Colours

It's recommend to use intarsia style colour work for this project and colour changes should be made in the stitch before the new colour is required, by completing the last stitch in the new colour.

There is no need to cut or fasten off the yarn when not in use, simply leave the unworked yarn on the **WS** of the project, at the last worked stitch and pick it up when needed, ensuring there is no pulling or tension on the yarn to work it in the rest of the round.

Example - Round 17, 30th Stitch
- Insert hook in 30th stitch
- In original colour (Red), Yarn over, bring up a loop
- Change to White
- Yarn over, pull through 2 loops
- Continue working next stitch in the new colour

Pattern - Base

Round 1: With **A**, make MC (or ch 4, sl st to 1st to create a ring), 6 sc into the centre of ring, sl st to 1st sc to join - 6 sc

Round 2: Ch 1 (does not count), 2sc in same as ch 1 and each around, join - 12 sc

Round 3: Ch 1, *sc, 2sc in next; repeat from * to end, join - 18 sc

Round 4: Ch 1, *sc in next 2, 2sc in next; repeat from * to end, join - 24 sc

Round 5: Ch 1, *sc in next 3, 2sc in next; repeat from * to end, join - 30 sc

Round 6: Ch 1, *sc in next 4, 2sc in next; repeat from * to end, join - 36 sc

Round 7: Ch 1, *sc in next 5, 2sc in next; repeat from * to end, join - 42 sc

Round 8: Ch 1, sc in next 3, *2sc in next, sc in next 6*, repeat from * to last 3, sc in last 3, join - 48 sc

Round 9: Ch 1, *sc in next 7, 2sc into next*; repeat from * to end, join - 54 sc

Round 10: Ch 1, sc in next 4, *2sc in next, sc in next 8; repeat from * to last 4, sc in last 4, join - 60 sc

Round 11: Ch 1, *sc in next 9, 2 sc into next, repeat from* to end, join - 66 sc

Round 12: Ch 1, *working in BLO,* sc each around, join - 66 sc

Rounds 13-14: With **C,** ch 1, sc in each around, join

Rounds 15-16: With **A,** ch 1, sc in each around, join

Round 17: Ch 1, sc in next 30, with **D**, *working in BLO,* sc in next 5, with **A**, sc in each around to end, join

Round 18: Ch 1, sc in next 27, with **D**, *working in BLO,* sc in next 5, with **A**, sc in each around to end, join

Round 19: Ch 1, sc in next 25, with **D**, sc in BLO of next 15, with **A**, sc in each around to end, join

Round 20: With **D**, ch 1, *working into BLO around,* sc in next 31, hdc in next, dc in next, hdc in next, sc in each around to end, join

Round 21: Continuing with **D**, ch 1, *working in BLO,* sc in next 25, *working through both loops of stitch,* with **B**, sc in next 2, hdc in next, dc in next 2, hdc in next, sc in next 3, hdc in next, dc in next 2, hdc in next, sc in next 2, with **D,** *working in BLO,* sc in each to end, join

Round 22: Ch 1, *working in BLO,* hdc in next 24, with **B**, *working through both loops of stitch,* dc in next 3, sc in next 11, hdc in next 3, with **D**, *working in BLO,* hdc in each to end, join

Round 23: Ch 1, *working in BLO,* sc next 24, with **B**, *working through both loops of stitch,* sc in next 17, with **D**, *working in BLO,* sc in each to end, join

Round 24: Ch 1, *working in BLO,* sc in each around, join

Rounds 25-26: With **A**, ch 1, *working in BLO,* sc in each around, join

Round 27: Ch 1, skip st under ch, sc in each remaining st around, join - 65 sc

Round 28: Repeat Round 27 - 64 sc

Rounds 29-37: Ch 1, sc in each around, join

Fasten off after Round 37. Weave ends
Fold at row 25 and tuck inside

Adding Santa's Face

Santa's Eyes
- Thread the darning needle with black yarn
- Bring needle through wrong through top of sc in Round 22, above the 2 dc in Round 21
- Insert the needle through top of dc in Round 21
- Repeat sewing in same, 3 times, to create an eye
- Repeat for second eye

Fasten off and secure ends

Santa's Nose
- Thread the darning needle with pink
- Bring needle through from wrong side, at the start of the 3 taller stitches (hdc, dc, hdc) in Round 20
- Insert needle back to wrong side through last hdc, to cover the 3 taller stitches
- Sew over and around the group of stitches 4 times to create his nose

Fasten off and secure ends

Santa's Jaunty Smile
- Thread the darning needle with red yarn
- Bring needle through from wrong side, 1 row, and 1 stitch lower than corner of nose
- Insert needle through stitch 2 rows down from middle of nose, bring needle from back to come out through sc 1 row above the top of the mouth
- Reinsert needle 2 rows down, through the middle of the sc
- Repeat positioning for the bottom of the smile

Fasten off and secure ends

Pattern - Pom-Pom

You can choose to make a traditional pom-pom using yarn or create a crochet ball using the optional Snuggly Snowflake and **5mm hook**, or holding 2 strands of White together

Round 1: Make MC (or ch 4, sl st to 1st to create ring), ch 1, 8 hdc in centre of ring, join - 8 hdc

Round 2: Ch 1, 2hdc in each around, join - 16 hdc

Round 3: Ch 1, hdc2tog in each around, join - 8 hdc
Stuff firmly with toy stuffing
Fasten off with long tail and use tail to weave through each st to close

Pattern - Lid

Round 1: With **A**, make MC (or ch 4, sl st to creat a ring), 6sc into the centre of the ring, sl st to 1st sc to join - 6 sc

Round 2: Ch 1, 2sc in same as ch 1 and each around, join - 12 sc

Round 3: Ch 1, *sc, 2sc in next; repeat from * to end, join - 18 sc

Round 4: Ch 1, *sc in next 2, 2sc in next; repeat from * to end, join 24 sc

Round 5: Ch 1, *sc in next 3, 2sc in next; repeat from * to end, join - 30 sc

Round 6: Ch 1, *sc in next 4, 2sc in next; repeat from * to end, join - 36 sc

Round 7: Ch 1, sc in each around, join - 36 sc

Round 8: Ch 1, *sc in next 5, 2sc in next; repeat from * to end, join - 42 sc

Round 9: Ch 1, sc in each around, join - 42 sc

Round 10: Ch 1, sc in next 3, *2sc in next, sc in next 6; repeat from * to last 3, sc in last 3, join - 48 sc

Round 11: Ch 1, *sc in next 7, 2sc into next; repeat from * to end, join - 54 sc

Round 12: Ch 1, sc in each around, join - 54 sc

Round 13: Ch 1, sc in next 4, *2sc in next, sc in next 8; repeat from * to last 4, sc in last 4, join - 60 sc

Round 14: Ch 1, *sc in next 9, 2 sc into next; repeat from * to end, join - 66 sc

Attach Pompom through Round 1, with **RS** facing

Round 15: With **D**, ch 1, *working in BLO,* sc in each around, join - 66 sc

Round 16: Ch 1, *sc in next 9, sc2tog across next 2, repeat from * to end, join - 60 sc

Round 17: Ch 1, sc in next 4, *sc2tog across next 2, sc in next 8; repeat from * to last 6, sc2tog across next 2, sc in last 4, join - 54 sc

Round 18: Ch 1, *sc in next 7, sc2tog across next 2; repeat from * to end, join - 48 sc

Round 19: Ch 1, *sc in next 6 , sc2tog across next 2; repeat from * to end, join - 42 sc

Round 20: Ch 1, *sc in next 5, sc2tog across next 2; repeat from * to end, join - 36 sc

Round 21: Ch 1, *sc in next 4, sc2tog across next 2; repeat from * to end, join, - 30 sc

Round 22: Ch 1 *sc in next 3, sc2tog across next 2; repeat from * to end, join - 24 sc

Round 23: Ch 1, *sc in next 2, sc2tog across next 2; repeat from * to end, join - 18 sc

Round 24: Ch 1, *sc in next, sc2tog across next 2; repeat from * to end, join - 12 sc

Stuff Lid with toy stuffing

Round 25: Ch 1, sc2tog around, join - 6 sc

Fasten off with long tail.
Use tail to weave through sts to close
Weave in remaining ends

Christmas Tree Coaster

Christmas is all about getting together with those that you love, and a steaming mug of hot chocolate or a mulled wine, which can only lead to lots of good times. These coasters are perfect to set your mugs upon while you take a moment to chat between sips.

Pattern Notes

- This coaster is worked in turned rows
- **A** will be carried and worked over when not in use
- **B** can be picked up to work with on the return row
- Colour should be changed after Bean is completed, and counts as ch 1

Finished Size

5 inches square

Special Stitch

Bean = Bean Stitch
- Insert hook in stitch indicated, YO, bring up loop, YO, insert hook into same, YO, bring up loop, YO, pull through all 4 loops on hook, ch 1 to complete
    - Mini Bean is worked in space at side of Bean from previous round/row

Materials

- Any chunky/Size 5 yarn
- I used Paintbox Yarns Simply Chunky (100g/3.5oz 136m/149yd) in 3 shades:
    - **A** - Champagne White (302)
    - **B** - Washed Teal (332)
    - **C** - Light Caramel (308)
- 6mm crochet hook
- Darning needle
- Scissors

Pattern

Row 1: With **A**, ch 19, in 3rd ch from hook (skipped chs count as sc, ch 1), *Bean, skip next ch; repeat from * across to end, turn - 9 Bean, 1 sc

Row 2: Ch 2 (count as sc, ch 1), Bean in next 4 ch-1 sps, with **B**, Bean in next ch-1 sp, with **A**, Bean in last 4 ch-1 sps, turn

Row 3: Ch 2, Bean in next 3 ch-1 sps, with **B**, Bean in next 2 ch-1 sps, with **A**, Bean in last 4 ch-1 sps, turn

Row 4: Ch 2, Bean in next 3 ch-1 sps, with **B**, Bean in next 3 ch-1 sps, with **A**, Bean in last 3 ch-1 sps, turn

Row 5: Ch 2, Bean in next 2 ch-1 sps, with **B**, Bean in next 4 ch-1 sps, with **A**, Bean in last 3 ch-1 sps, turn

Row 6: Ch 2, Bean in next 2 ch-1 sps, with **B**, Bean in next 5 ch-1 sps, with **A**, Bean in last 2 ch-1 sps, turn

Row 7: Ch 2, Bean in next ch-1 sp, with **B**, Bean in next 6 ch-1 sps, with **A**, Bean in last 2 ch-1 sps, turn

Row 8: Ch 2, Bean in next ch-1 sp, with **A**, Bean in next 7 ch-1 sps, with **A**, Bean in last ch-1 sp, turn

Row 9: Ch 2, Bean in next 3 ch-1 sps, with **C**, Bean in next 2 ch-1 sps, with **A**, Bean in last 4 ch-1 sps, turn

Row 10: Ch 2, Bean in next 4 ch-1 sps, with **C**, Bean in next ch-1 sp, with **A**, Bean in last 4 ch-1 sps, turn

Row 11: Ch 2, Bean in each ch-1 sp across
Fasten off, weave in all ends

Christmas Tree Mug Cosy

This pattern uses the same special stitch as the Christmas Tree Coaster, but is designed to fit the whole mug inside to help keep that hot chocolate warmer for longer.

This quick festive project can be used to spice up a quick gift idea, by adding it to a new mug alongside some tasty hot chocolate supplies.

Pattern Notes

- The base of the mug cosy is worked in joined rounds **and** turned rounds, the sides are worked in turned rows
- It is recommended to carry the unworked yarn on the wrong side (inside of the cosy)
- Colour should be changed after Bean is completed, and counts as ch 1

Special Stitch

Bean = Bean Stitch
- Insert hook in stitch indicated, YO, bring up loop, YO, insert hook into same, YO, bring up loop, YO, pull through all 4 loops on hook, ch 1 to complete
- Mini Bean is worked in space at side of Bean from previous round/row

Finished Size

To fit standard mug

Materials

- Any Aran/Worsted acrylic yarn
- I used Designer used Paintbox Yarns Simply Aran (100g/3.5oz 184m)
    - **A** – 40m Champagne White (202)
    - **B** – 25m Pistachio (224)
- 5mm crochet hook
- Darning needle
- Scissors
- 2 x 7mm invisible snap fasteners

Pattern

Round 1: With **A**, ch 4, sl st to 1st ch to create ring, ch 1, *working in centre of ring*, 8 hdc, join – 8 hdc

Round 2: Ch 1 (does not count), 2hdc in each around, join – 16 hdc

Round 3: Ch 1, *hdc in next, 2hdc in next; repeat from * around, join – 24 hdc

Round 4: Ch 1, *hdc in next 2, 2hdc in next; repeat from * around, join – 32 hdc

Round 5: Ch 1, *hdc in next 3, 2hdc in next; repeat from * around, join – 40 hdc

Round 6: Ch 1, *Bean in next, skip next; repeat from * around, join, **turn** – 20 Bean, 20 ch-1 sp *(from closing Bean st)*

Round 7: Ch 1, Bean in ch-1 sp under join, skip ch-1 sp, *Bean in next, skip ch-1 sp; repeat from * around, join, **turn** - 20 Bean, 20 ch-1 sp

Begin working in rows

Row 1: Ch 1, hdc in same as join, ch 1, skip ch-1 sp, Bean in next ch-1 sp (see photo below), *Bean in next, skip ch-1 sp; repeat from * 17 times, until last 2 Beans, hdc in ch-1 sp (see photo below), leave remaining Beans unworked, **turn** – 18 Bean, 2 hdc

Row 2: Ch 1, hdc in same, ch 1, skip ch-1 sp, with **B**, [Bean in next, skip ch-1 sp] 7 times, with **A**, [Bean in next, skip ch-1 sp] 4 times, with **B**, [Bean in next, skip ch-1 sp] 7 times, with **A**, hdc in last, turn. **A** - 4 Beans, 2 hdc, **B** - 14 Beans

Row 3: Continuing with **A**, Ch 1, hdc in same, ch 1, skip ch-1 sp, with **B**, [Bean in next, skip ch-1 sp] 6 times, with **A**, [Bean in next, skip ch-1 sp] 5 times, with **B**, [Bean in next, skip ch-1 sp] 6 times, with **A**, [Bean in next, skip ch-1 sp], hdc in last, ch 6, turn. **A** - 6 Beans, 2 hdc, **B** - 12 Beans, ch 6

Row 4: Continuing with **A**, *working back down ch,* hdc in 2nd ch from hook and next 4 ch, hdc in next, ch 1, skip ch-1 sp, [Bean in next, skip ch-1 sp], with **B**, [Bean in next, skip ch-1 sp] 5 times, with **A**, [Bean in next, skip ch-1 sp] 6 times, with **B**, [Bean in next, skip ch-1 sp] 5 times, with **A**, [Bean in next, skip ch-1 sp], hdc in last, turn. **A** - 8 Beans, 2 hdc, **B** - 10 Beans

Row 5: Continuing with **A,** ch 1, hdc in same, ch 1, skip ch-1 sp, [Bean in next, skip ch-1 sp], with **B**, [Bean in next, skip ch-1 sp] 4 times, with **A**, [Bean in next, skip ch-1 sp] 7 times, with **B**, [Bean in next, skip ch-1 sp] 4 times, with **A**, [Bean in next, skip ch-1 sp] 2 times, hdc in next, leave remaining sts unworked, turn. **A** – 10 Beans, 2 hdc, **B** - 8 Beans

Row 6: Continuing with **A,** ch 1, hdc in same, ch 1, [Bean in next, skip ch-1 sp] 2 times, with **B**, [Bean in next, skip ch-1 sp] 3 times, with **A**, [Bean in next, skip ch-1 sp] 8 times, with **B**, [Bean in next, skip ch-1 sp] 3 times, with **A**, [Bean in next, skip ch-1 sp] 2 times hdc in last, turn. **A** – 12 Beans, 2 hdc, **B** - 6 Beans

Row 7: Continuing with **A,** ch 1, hdc in same, ch 1, skip ch-1 sp, [Bean in next, skip ch-1 sp] 2 times, with **B**, [Bean in next, skip ch-1 sp] 2 times, with **A**, [Bean in next, skip ch-1 sp] 9 times, with **B**, [Bean in next, skip ch-1 sp] 2 times, with **A**, [Bean in next, skip ch-1 sp] 3 times hdc in last, turn. **A** – 14 Beans, 2 hdc, **B** - 4 Beans

Row 8: Continuing with **A,** ch 1, hdc in same, ch 1, skip ch-1 sp, [Bean in next, skip ch-1 sp] 3 times, with **B**, [Bean in next, skip ch-1 sp], with **A**, [Bean in next, skip ch-1 sp] 10 times, with **B**, [Bean in next, skip ch-1 sp], with **A**, [Bean in next, skip ch-1 sp] 3 times, hdc in last, turn. **A** – 16 Beans, 2 hdc, **B** - 2 Beans

Row 9: Continuing with **A,** ch 1, hdc in same, ch 1, skip ch-1 sp, [Bean in next, skip ch-1 sp] in each across to last, hdc in last, ch 6, turn. **A** – 18 Beans, 2 hdc, 6 ch

Row 10: *working back down ch,* sc in 2nd ch from hook and next 4 ch, sc in next st and each ch-1 sp and Bean across to end, sc in last -44 sc
Fasten off, weave ends

Attach snap fasteners to tabs to secure mug cosy around handle

Acknowledgments

With you I am something, but together, we are everything!

This quote features in all of my crochet pattern books, simply because it captures how I feel about the wonderful crochet community we are all a part of and I am so grateful to have you as a part of it.

I want to thank you from the bottom of stocking for choosing to spend your crochet time making one of my festive patterns - I'd really love to see a photo of your completed projects.

I always want to extend my thanks to all of my crafty, crochet cheerleaders too; I see you there, stitching away, watching my videos, commenting and sharing my patterns and pictures and I love you for it.

A special thank you goes to my one of my crochet besties, Julie - without her hard working hands and her endless support, this book would never have been completed. There are a number of her beautiful projects that feature in the photos in this book. I'm eternally grateful for her being so generous with her time and friendship. I look forward to our Wednesday afternoon crochet sessions.

Another special thank you is to the Fibre Arts Friends group that meet twice monthly in Duston. The granny's baubles pictured in this book have been stitched up by their fair hands so I can feature their crochet skills in this book too. So, thank you to Julie, Nicky and Angie, Sue S, Sue E, Maddie, Tish and Deb, Elaine, Faye, Maggie, Deb, Donna, and Fiona M

As always, I can't forget to thank my lovely husband, who is also as big a Christmas Lover as I am - lucky really, as he's the only one who hang the giant wreath on the house and fully supports buying a new supersized outside decoration each year! Thank you as always for everything you've done for me, and continue to do to let me play with yarn so much.

Keep in Touch!

In this day and age, it's easy to make and move on, but you're part of the Cosy Community now, so come and say hi!

 CosyRosieCrochet

 CosyRosieUK

 CosyRosieUK

 Scan for website

Resources

Yarn
PaintBox Yarns - www.lovecrafts.com
Hayfield Bonus - Sirdar.com
WI Premium Acrylic DK - hobbycraft.co.uk
Rico Creative Cotton - rico-design.de
Brava Worsted - crochet.com

Hooks
We all have our favourite hooks, and some of mine have featured in the photography in this book:
1. Furls Crochet Wooden Streamline - www.furlscrochet.com
2. Pony Soft Grip Crochet Hook - www.hobbycraft.co.uk

Photography
A huge thank you to Khandie for the super pretty photography and being so excited for the holidays
www.khandiephotography.com